FROM TALKING

TO

DOING

A Short Guide to

Corporate Innovation Success

JOYCE J. SHEN

Printed in the United States of America

First Printing 2019

10 9 8 7 6 5 4 3 2 1

ISBN: 978-1-7329558-0-6

For my parents

CONTENTS

Acknowledgements

Introduction   i

1. What is Innovation with Outcomes?   1

2. Types of Outcomes for Innovation Projects   15

3. Should You Build a Corporate Venture Capital Group?   30

4. How to Build Organizational Capability for Innovation?   45

5. Employee Development & Building Innovation Culture   69

6. Keep It Simple   80

7. Building a Business is Running a Marathon   83

8. Managing Chaos   88

9. Checklist for Success   93

About the Author   99

Index   100

ACKNOWLEDGEMENTS

I have wanted to write this book for a long time so that I can share what I have learned first-hand with others who also want to succeed in building innovation for companies. It is one thing for people to talk about building innovation, while it is another to have the opportunity to actually do it and overcome challenges to make corporate innovation succeed at scale. I want to thank my colleagues and friends. I am inspired by them every day through their leadership, creativity, and generosity.

INTRODUCTION

Much has been written about innovation. Most of the writings, often from theoretical perspectives, cover general approaches and introduce types of innovation—architectural innovation, creative innovation, incremental innovation, disruptive innovation. The list goes on.

While it is important to understand the theoretical concepts to jumpstart innovation building, I would argue that in practice, innovation framework with strong bent on clarification of outcomes and implementation is much more essential for an organization.

Innovation with outcomes is designed to:

- Help corporate executives and intrapreneurs in medium and large organizations to become strategically "street smart" and more effective in actually delivering innovation.

- Minimize significant upfront investments to build an innovation engine.

- Create a forward-looking path to enable longer term replicability and sustainability of innovation projects.

As we know, innovation is hard and messy because in reality innovation is not just about ripping out the legacy and replacing with the new. Corporate executives and intrapreneurs understand this fact because they are in the trenches of complex organizations that generate billions of revenues every quarter. Innovating in these organizations is not turning a switch. I understand this because I was also there as an intrapreneur and a builder—building IBM's mergers & acquisitions capabilities, building IBM's Cloud Platform-as-a-Service in a shifting enterprise software and cloud landscape, and building Thomson Reuters' emerging technologies innovation, partnerships, and venture investment fund in a shifting big data and artificial intelligence landscape.

Beyond intrapreneurs who have the mandate to build innovation capabilities inside organizations, Board of Directors, Chief Executive Officer, Chief Financial Officer, Chief Operating Officer, Chief Innovation Officer, and Chief Technology Officer also need an outcome-based innovation framework that can truly enable them and help organizations deliver on the expected return of investment on innovation project.

CHAPTER 1

WHAT IS INNOVATION WITH OUTCOMES?

Outcome-based innovation is creating and defining innovation programs and projects based on clear business outcomes that are strategically aligned to the organization.

Is the innovation project essential to the business? What are the desired outcomes? Why are they desirable for the organization? One should ask these questions before embarking on an innovation project.

Far too often, innovation in a large organization takes place because the organization has an interest to check a box. Without a clear definition of an outcome, the innovation project is destined to fail or at best to become a "window dressing" project. Even worse, innovation projects or programs that are funded without clear orientation toward their outcomes are often eliminated first when organizations need to tighten up budget to weather business headwinds.

As a reality, outcome-based innovation is much more sustainable and shields teams who work on innovation projects from the pendulum of corporate budgeting.

To further unpack outcome-based innovation framework, we see the following benefits when this framework is deployed:

- Increase probability of success of innovation projects.

- Implicitly require a set of processes and capabilities that would bring advantages to the broader organization.

- Generate tangible and differentiated thought leadership for the organization.

How to increase probability of success in the delivery of innovation projects? In my experience, beyond having good ideas, the ability to systematically unpack ideas is key to increase this probability of success.

Put in simple terms, the "unpacking of the idea" process includes three table stakes: validation, clarification, and synchronization.

These three table stakes set up the outcome-based innovation framework.

Validation

First, in a matrixed organization, validating an idea calls for talking to functional leaders in finance, marketing, sales as well as key stakeholders working in other business segments. This step is important to shape the type of outcome that matters not only to the immediate team or business segment but also to the broader organization.

Second, validating an idea calls for talking with potential customers—whether the customer is external or internal to the organization. A key question to ask here: what value could the innovation project deliver to that intended customer? The value could be in the form of market insights to a proof-of-concept of a new idea to the launch of a new product.

Third, validating an idea calls for surveying existing products or solutions, internal or external, which may provide similar functionality or outcome. Even if a similar idea exists or has been raised before, validation is needed. This does not mean that the current idea would not be impactful. The team has to do the homework to validate where and how this new innovation idea is positioned relative to the current universe of similar products or ideas.

Validation helps avoid tunnel vision, group think, and confirmation bias. Validation forces an individual or a team that is passionate about an innovation idea to become grounded in critical thinking and in understanding for whom this innovation idea will drive value and what makes the idea differentiated to the degree so that it is worth investing in.

The validation process functions as a channel of feedback from internal stakeholders, and these early feedbacks will be important in the synchronization phase.

Clarification

Clarification, while it seems similar to validation, is a distinct process and the second table stake in our framework.

Once an idea is validated through feedback and research, the next step is to ask the team to further clarify additional details of the idea to ensure that the team has done sufficient reflection to have a very clear view not only on why the idea is worth pursuing and investing in but also on the initial use case for constructing the minimal viable product (MVP).

Whether it is an idea for consumers or an idea for business users, clarify the initial use case. Specifically, a use case is how an idea would be applied by the end user for a particularly strong purpose or solve one of the most pressing user pain points. The team should identify specific workflow for which the idea can add clear utility. Here are some questions to ask during this clarification step:

- What is the workflow that enables the completion of a mission-critical process?

- What are the elements in the workflow that are causing friction, inconvenience, inefficiencies, additional costs, or end user dissatisfaction and why?

- How would the idea be translated into functionalities and capabilities that would drive utility in the workflow to reduce inefficiencies and dissatisfaction?

- Which type of end user would be the most willing persona to apply the idea and to experiment with the new functionalities and capabilities?

If the team can articulate clear answers to the questions such as the above, then the team will have clarified to themselves and to others about the use case and will have further made the idea more tangible to pave a path for methodical delivery.

The use case development and in turn initial product market fit start by answering the above questions. Then, the translation of the answers into initial product features are essential in establishing a foundational view of the minimal viable product. Reversely, a common pitfall associated with the minimal viable product is generality and lack of clarification—without constructing details of a use case to truly reflect the features and functions needed by the targeted users.

To sum up, validation helps declare whether the idea is legit and has a potential market opportunity to invest time and resources. Clarification helps develop the details of a use case and further hone-in-on the product market fit.

Synchronization

Synchronization is the third table stake in the process to unpack innovation ideas effectively.

In addition to validating an idea and clarifying initial use case to pave the way for minimal viable product, synchronization ensures that an individual or an innovation team perform necessary analysis and build a project and product plan that is operationally sound and achievable.

As the name of this step suggests, synchronization is to "pull it together." Sounds obvious, but in an organizational setting, this step generally poses a big challenge and is complex to achieve. The lack of synchronization often causes innovation projects to go sideways and fail in the long-term.

Synchronization calls for an individual or a team with the innovation idea to establish a concrete implementation plan with consensus built in. Building the said plan is to operationalize the initial minimal viable product. The plan is both a project and a product plan (yes, even for an MVP) that breaks down innovation project execution into blocks of tactical work required and helps set strategic goal posts.

Key elements to synchronize and build the project and product plans:

Sponsor of the Innovation Project

- Is the project and financial sponsor from a corporate function, or a technology organization or a business unit?
- Is the project and financial sponsor the same individual? If not, has the team synchronized goals and objectives of the respective sponsors?

- Has the business outcome of the innovation project been validated and clarified, aligning with long-term value creation of the sponsor and broader organization?

- If diverging views exist in the organization, how can the innovation team find shared interest and common goals to achieve alignment with the various perspectives in the organization to ensure that the innovation project is not replicated or become detoured in another part of the organization?

Product Management of the Innovation Project

- After the clarification stage, is an individual with product management experience identified and put in place to translate the use case into features and functions of the minimal viable product to create a blueprint for software developers and engineers?

- Does this said individual have the ability to continuously evaluate the minimal viable product for product market fit against existing product portfolio to demonstrate the net new positive impact from the innovation idea?

Project Delivery Questions for the Innovation Project

- Has the team secured financial funding for the initial phase of the project?

- If the innovation team cannot hire full-time individuals, how is the team crowdsourcing talents from other teams in the rest of the organization?

- How does the innovation team create an incentive structure to make sure that other teams in the organization that are contributing talent resources also feel accountable for the success of the outcome?

- Has the organization appointed a project manager?

- Does this individual possess the multi-dimensional skills to manage an innovation project from recruiting resources to negotiating with internal stakeholders to working with other innovators to execute the project on time and to performance target?

- Has the team explored long-term funding model of the project once the initial MVP will be completed?

- Is the innovation project going to be incorporated in an existing business or product or is the innovation project going to become the basis of a standalone new product or initiative?

- What is the project collaboration model among various functions from project management to product management to engineering?

- What are the operating rhythm and goal posts to measure progress and performance of the team in aggregate and on an individual level?

These questions on long-term sponsorship, funding, resource, and success metrics should be brought up proactively at the beginning of the innovation project and must be explored as part of the synchronization process. This way, the innovation team will have better chance to ensure that the project has sufficient support to start, to continue, and to potentially move into a scalable mode.

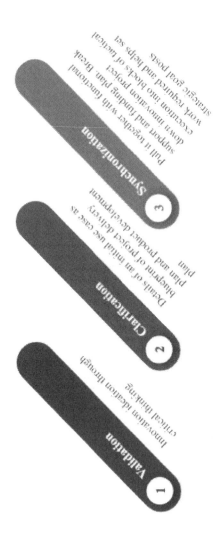

CHAPTER 2

TYPES OF OUTCOMES FOR INNOVATION PROJECTS

Before we dive into organizational capabilities that would empower end-to-end innovation in a large organization, let us first dissect the different types of outcomes from innovation projects. We want to innovate to create value. So we must understand the outcomes that we desire. Then we can create clear plans to achieve these outcomes.

Organizations with a clear sense of the objectives for innovation projects will innovate more effectively. CEOs and line-of-business owners are more likely to support innovation projects that have gone through a thorough process of validation, clarification, and synchronization because this process helps generate clear and accountable thinking and planning.

Most organizations want to achieve a number of outcomes from innovation projects. Therefore, the first step is to identify the main outcome that an organization cares most about from an innovation project. The motivation and objectives of innovation projects generally fall under one of the five categories of outcomes, as outlined below:

1. *Develop and launch new product in an existing served market.*

2. *Develop and launch the new product in an adjacent or new market.*

3. *Improve existing process or create a new process to fill a gap.*

4. *Strengthen thought leadership.*

5. *Build talent pipeline and retain talent.*

The first two outcomes, centered around product development, are strategic and go-to-market in nature. The last three outcomes, centered around processes and practices that make organizations run and empowered, are tactical and operational in nature.

For each of the outcomes above, we will methodically unpack and analyze what each outcome means from a variety of dimensions: definition and objective, success measurement, and the long-term success framework.

1. Develop and launch new product in an existing served market

Definition and Objective

The company wants to create and launch a new product (not feature of a product) to sell to existing served industries and customers.

The objective of the innovation is to effectively identify a new product area that meets a specific need of existing customers that are willing to pay more for the new product. Acquisition is not necessarily a feasible route. Therefore, organic product innovation becomes the primary tool to explore.

Success Measurement

Launch of the new product.

Continuous customer feedback.

Funding plan. Continued budget and funding to support and sustain the distribution and product roadmap of the new product.

Long-term Success Framework

Use the Validation-Clarification-Synchronization framework to ensure that the new product idea is sound.

Build bottoms-up business case for funding needs, hiring needs, and business milestones.

Conduct the discussion with CFO early and identify budget source in the short term and long term.

Identify sources of talent and develop a recruiting strategy to attract and hire the right talent to build a lean team. Build organizational support across functional areas early in order to establish important buy-in and roadmap for sustained product launch and development.

Establish market development strategy and implementation plan to gain mindshare among existing customers that have an "early adopter" profile.

2. Develop and launch new product in an adjacent or new market

Definition and Objective

The company wants to create and launch a new product and sell to a new market (e.g., geography, vertical).

The objective of the innovation is to identify a new product that can effectively help the company establish footprint in a new market, whether it is in a new geography or in a new industry. The new product and the business infrastructure and capabilities for the new product can also serve as an overall launchpad for new market expansion.

New product innovation in an adjacent or a new market is an organic approach that is utilized after concluding that inorganic activity (mergers and acquisitions) is not a more efficient route to establish footprint and expansion in an adjacent or a new market.

Success Measurement

Launch of the new product.

Early customer feedback.

Milestones and risk mitigators to track when to stop the innovation efforts or when to accelerate the efforts to capture market opportunity with early positive market signals. Capital plan to support and sustain product roadmap, new market development, and expansion.

Long term Success Framework

Use the Validation-Clarification-Synchronization framework to ensure that the market assessment and new product idea are sound.

Build bottoms-up business case for funding needs, hiring needs, and business milestones. Build enterprise risk plan to track the innovation project to decide when to stop funding and when to accelerate.

Conduct early discussion with CEO, CFO, and leaders in related markets (geography and vertical) to obtain and strengthen tangible support. Identify budget source in short term and long term for product and operational costs that come with new market development and expansion. Identify sources of talent and develop recruiting strategy to land the right individuals to build a lean, diverse, and highly capable team with product, geography, industry, and commercial expertise. Build organizational support across functional areas early in order to establish the important buy-in and roadmap for sustained product launch and development.

Establish market development strategy and implementation plan to gain mindshare among existing customers that have an "early adopter" profile.

3. Improve existing process or create a new process to fill a gap

Definition and Objective

The company wants to transform existing processes of various departments and functional areas and potentially change the existing way of doing things.

The objective of the innovation is to identify and implement changes or alternatives to existing processes to reduce inefficiency in a complex system and optimize the allocations of the same set of resources and investments across the organization.

Success Measurement

Clearly identify and validate bottlenecks in the process within the system.

Obtain internal and/or customer feedback on drivers or root causes of inefficiency. Effectively incorporate these feedbacks into the process redesign.

Establish clear ways to measure efficiency gains of the new process to demonstrate impact of the outcome.

Devise specific ways and assign stakeholders to continue to iterate on the process changes in the complex system.

Long term Success Framework

Use the Validation Clarification Synchronization framework. Build bottoms-up business case to illustrate incremental value that can be and will be generated by innovation in business processes.

Ensure that the implementation of the process improvement and innovation is mapped to a set of key stakeholders and individuals who will own and drive the process forward.

Find ways to incorporate lessons learned from this innovation process into other existing business processes and risk management programs where applicable.

Gain CFO or VP of Finance's trust and approval and make this key stakeholder a champion and sponsor of the innovation project.

4. Strengthen thought leadership

Definition and Objective

The company wants to establish or strengthen its voice and perspective on a specific topic so that external markets know that the organization has a strong and informed view backed by its experience and track record.

The objective of the innovation is to build the company's knowledge and harness its existing expertise in a particular topic and use various channels to establish or amplify thought leadership.

Success Measurement

Clearly identify the topics or related topics that the organization wants to achieve for thought leadership. Ensure that the organization has available intellectual property assets to support the thought leadership.

Ensure that there are partners in corporate communications and corporate affairs teams to support this innovation project.

In addition to traditional metrics (e.g., number of page views, clicks, impressions), establish business metrics that can be enabled by thought leadership. Weave thought leadership into market-building activities and ensure the innovation project in building thought leadership that is outcome-based and grounded.

Market-building activities include general business development, market development, and client insights.

Long term Success Framework

Use the Validation Clarification Synchronization framework to ensure that the process innovation idea would indeed be valuable and can deliver more than incremental value.

Ensure that thought leadership is part of the business goal, not just another goal of corporate communication, marketing, or strategy teams. The product team has as much responsibility to build thought leadership as the marketing team does. The teams have to work collaboratively.

Outcomes that can be derived from innovation in thought leadership should be defined clearly in annual performance measurement across relevant teams in the organization.

In addition to the CEO, bring CFO or VP of Finance along as trusted advisor, champion, and sponsor of this innovation.

5. Build talent pipeline and retain talent

Definition and Objective

The company wants to establish a pipeline of candidates to stay competitive with its peers or to be able to expand into new markets.

The objective of this innovation is to work across the organization to identify areas to build talent pipeline and apply various recruiting approaches to ensure that the organization is competitive in the eyes of the best talents.

Success Measurement

A talent acquisition and retention strategy co-created by Human Resources, Corporate Strategy,

Finance, and Line of Business owners (e.g., CTO, business unit general managers, research leaders).

- Start with business and technology strategy for next 3, 5, 10 years.

- Identify key skills for next generation of leaders. Those individuals who possess skills to become next general of leaders may not look like leaders of today. Business and HR teams should have a way to debias.

- Identify specific channels to identify and recruit new talents.

Develop a holistic evaluation framework that assesses both quantitative and qualitative aspects of the candidates. Develop end-to-end talent acquisition and retention metrics.

Long term Success Framework

Long term success framework for building talent pipeline and retaining those talent requires organizations to rethink Human Resources as it stands today. Human Resources is a function, not a strategy.

To compete in today's marketplace, organizations need to build the talent acquisition and retention strategy by first developing business and technology strategy that can be effectively communicated to HR partners.

Business leaders and HR teams need to work together to develop a repeatable way to find emerging skills that might become a competitive advantage for the business. Creating this linkage in the organization is a must, but it is often ignored or overlooked.

CHAPTER 3

SHOULD YOU BUILD A CORPORATE VENTURE CAPITAL GROUP?

Many case studies have been written about corporate ventures such as Google Ventures, Intel Capital, and strategic investment arms of financial institutions. This chapter is not documenting these corporate venture examples but rather providing strategic and practical framework to enable corporate innovation and intrapreneurs, so that corporate venture can play an accelerant role.

No doubt, a re-emerging trend is the rise of corporate venture capital. But is it right for most organizations? And if corporate venture is a strategically viable element to corporate innovation, then how does an organization and its intrapreneurs build this capability? Before we discuss whether corporate venture is the right

model for an organization, let us lay out some
fundamental concepts.

Put in layman terms, corporate venture is
generally the process and mechanism that allow an
organization to make strategic minority
investment in an early or growth stage company.
The limited partner is generally the parent
organization.

Corporate venture requires strong long-term
strategic thesis and objectives to support the
investment thesis, which then guides the types of
investments that the organization would make.
Said differently, in corporate venture, financial
return is secondary to long-term strategic return
that is in the forms of revenue growth and
ultimately increase of shareholder value. In my
view, there are mainly two ways to organize
corporate venture—autonomous model and
embedded model.

Autonomous Model

Corporate ventures are structured in various ways. Some corporate venture teams have dedicated funds established as a separate pool of money without going through the standard corporate investment process to request funding whenever a validated investment opportunity arises. Distinctively, under an autonomous model, the investment team can approve the investments and execute on its own without additional corporate approval processes. This model provides autonomy of decision making for the corporate venture team as long as the investments align to the strategic investment thesis.

In the landscape of corporate venture, the autonomous corporate venture model is challenging to establish and sustain. A number of factors contribute to the difficulty of creating an autonomous model of corporate venture in an organization. Some common reasons include weak support from Board of Directors of the parent organization, lack of clarity in strategic focus and mandate, and lack of talent.

To sustain a dedicated fund structure and maintain autonomy of execution, the CEO and CFO of the organization have to be strong advocates. With strong advocacy from the CEO and CFO as well as with strong processes in place for accountability, the Board will more likely view corporate venture as an important strategic mandate supported by a detailed execution plan rather than a nice-to-have idea. This is key to sustained success of Intel Capital, Dell Ventures, and Google Ventures, for example. The senior management and the Board are aligned with the strategic purpose of why corporate venture exists, and the alignment engenders real tangible support through funding, Human Resources, and a clear autonomous model.

The second impediment to create a dedicated corporate venture fund is the lack of clarity on strategy. Venture investments are inherently risky.

For a corporation to create a dedicated fund and an autonomous model to invest in early and growth stage companies, the organization must have a very strong rationale to take this step. If investments do not meet expectations, the organization needs to be prepared to manage administrative cost and potentially reputational cost.

Corporate venture, unlike an institutional venture fund, often times cannot invest with a broad thesis because of lack of expertise. Institutional venture funds generally have expertise across industries and products, but corporate venture funds often cannot achieve this level of broad expertise because individuals running corporate ventures tend to be experts in the industries that the parent organization operates. Therefore, corporate venture needs strategic focus that maximizes the synergy that its investments can potential deliver to the organization—whether the synergy is accelerating product innovation, expanding distribution channel, or building a ripe pipeline for acquisitions.

The third impediment is the lack of talent. Corporate venture requires a bench of unique individuals to ensure its success in the long term. Unique talent generally needs to possess the ability as an investor and meanwhile as a strategic and operational influencer to operate within a large and complex organization.

The individuals with the right blend of transactional and operational experience are difficult to find, and most corporate venture usually has two types of individuals: individuals who predominantly invest and individuals who focus on operations of the corporate venture or on post-investment activities. Investors who are dealmakers often lack deep understanding of how to make a project work in a large organization, while operators typically cannot break into investor roles.

Often, internal candidates are hard to find. Many corporate development professionals have challenge succeeding in corporate venture because they either do not have the particular types of deal flow required for venture investments or cannot gain internal sponsorship to create the strategic alignment to execute the investments.

Another reason for lack of talent is misalignment in the compensation model. Most of the corporate ventures cannot or will not pay venture team in the same way as an institutional venture firm would pay its employees. Compensation in an institutional venture firm is largely based on performance of the investments. Because corporate venture's primary goal is mostly strategic return rather than financial return, there is limited upside in compensation. Best investors often gravitate to institutional funds.

At the same time, attracting external talent is not easy for corporate venture. It is not just about compensation. Most institutional investors fail at corporate venture because they lack organizational knowledge, credibility, or patience of investing inside a corporation compared to investing for a ten-year fund that has urgency to deploy its capital and reap return from a fund's best performing companies.

Embedded Model

For the reasons outlined above, most of the corporate venture activities are conducted through existing corporate investment process, often facilitated by the corporate development team. In general, when a venture investment opportunity arises, the investment will need to be approved through the existing corporate capital allocation process. This model of the corporate venture activity embedded in the existing corporate development process is often limiting.

Venture investments executed through the embedded model is often another execution path to get a transaction done, with usually the ultimate intent to acquire the company receiving the venture investment early on.

The first question then, for the innovator in the company, is whether this embedded model of the venture investments can still enable and empower outcome-based innovation in the expected timeframe and under the organizational framework.

As you can imagine, the answer to the above question depends on the outcome that the innovator intends to bring. In chapter 2 of this book, we discussed five types of outcomes:

1. *Develop and launch new product in an existing served market.*

2. *Develop and launch new product in an adjacent or new market.*

3. *Improve existing process or create a new process to fill a gap.*

4.   Strengthen thought leadership.

5.   Build talent pipeline and retain talent.

Among the five types of innovation-driven
outcomes, the embedded corporate venture model
would most effectively enable developing and
launching new products in an existing market and
strengthening thought leadership.

One main area that venture investments under the
embedded corporate venture model can make the
most impact is to accelerate new product in an
existing served market. The venture investment
can garner further corporate interest and
sponsorship in what the venture company is doing.
The intrapreneur, who is usually not the corporate
venture investor, needs to stay active and "plugged
in" with corporate venture activities at the
corporate level. And the intrapreneur needs to
constantly explore how he or she can translate and
transition a corporate venture investment into a

potentially meaningful product partnership to expand existing market share.

The second area that venture investment under the embedded corporate venture model can make a big impact is to strengthen thought leadership of an organization. Corporate venture is one form of "walking the talk" by an organization—actively participating in external innovation ecosystem and being a capital partner that has both strategic and economic interests in the portfolio companies. If the company can establish a methodical plan to link corporate venture activities to corporate communication, then the company can effectively communicate why the company is making venture investments from the lens of strategic alignment and long-term value creation.

Organizations with corporate venture missing this linkage between venture and communication will leave out an important opportunity to strengthen organizational thought leadership in the marketplace. Having strong and disciplined corporate communication to support corporate venture activities is essential to sustain a systematic way of seeding the innovation ecosystem. You would be surprised how many companies do not do a good job establishing this linkage and organizational capability.

Both autonomous and embedded corporate venture models are challenging to establish and maintain. But value creation could be enormous in the long-term if done right.

The above discussion highlights the two models.

As an intrapreneur, you should assess which of the two models is best suited for the organization and for the overall outcome-based innovation mandate. Once you decide on a model, then following the above discussion as an outline to draft a business plan. Now that we have a mental model of corporate venture, let's take a step back.

One of the first questions is whether corporate venture is a necessary and viable model. If you are an intrapreneur who wants to explore the creation of corporate venture, you must answer the following questions and write your business plan:

- Do you have corporate sponsorship from the CEO and CFO?

- Do you have functional sponsorship and support from Corporate Development, Accounting, Tax, Legal, Intellectual Property, Sales, Marketing, and Human Resources teams?

- Do you have the ability to establish an operating rhythm and model to gain feedback from the line of business and product teams on potential investment opportunities?

- Do you have a plan to "account manage" portfolio companies to report post-investment performance and manage post-investment activities including potential strategic partnerships with various stakeholders in the organization?

- Do you have the ability to generate a strong deal flow with companies of strong performance and alignment to strategic investment thesis?

If the answers to the above questions are mostly positive, then corporate venture could be a potentially viable model. The next set of actions is around "raising" the corporate fund and putting a business plan with execution details in place. If the answers to the above questions are mostly "no" or "maybe," then you are not ready to start a corporate venture in a serious and rigorous sense. More work is required to turn a "no" or a "maybe" to a "yes."

The additional work may be finding stronger sponsors, recruiting colleagues to be partners to ideate details of what a corporate venture would look like, and writing a more coherent business execution plan that is signed off by other internal key stakeholders who will support you in discussions with the CEO and CFO and help you execute the investments in the future.

Convincing a company to establish a corporate venture can often overlap with establishing organizational capabilities to develop and support a strong innovation ecosystem. We will discuss this topic in the next chapter.

CHAPTER 4

HOW TO BUILD ORGANIZATIONAL CAPABILITY FOR INNOVATION?

In this chapter, we explore key areas to build organizational capabilities to develop and support a strong innovation ecosystem. As discussed in the last chapter, the "how" and the results from a strong innovation ecosystem may pave the way for corporate venture if corporate venture would become another valuable lever in creating long-term value for the organization.

In any event, focusing on the right areas in building organizational capabilities is essential for any corporate innovation endeavors.

We again will offer practical guidance in this chapter, based on past experiences and lessons learned. We hope that with some of the learnings from this chapter, you can build your own organizational capabilities for innovation, know what to watch out for tactically and strategically, avoid costly pitfalls, and ultimately become an effective innovator with an enabling ecosystem around you inside your organization.

We will cover five most important areas of organizational capabilities: internal and external innovation, emerging technology strategy, new product incubation and development, market development, and making corporate process to engage with emerging technology companies startup friendly.

Internal and External Innovations

Successful corporate innovation requires both internal and external innovations.

Often, when organizations think about innovation, they arrive at either of the two perspectives: innovation is something that an organization must

do but with little distinction between internal and
external innovations. As a result, some
intrapreneurs are asked to focus on internal
innovation, while others are asked to build
external innovation ecosystem.

While the bifurcation of internal and external
innovation is needed, internal and external
innovations are naturally symbiotic and
synergistic. Both innovation approaches work
hand in hand. Let us first define and decipher
internal and external innovations.

Internal innovation is building organizational
capabilities inside the organization to enable any
one of the outcomes that this book discusses in
Chapter 3. These outcomes range from building
and launching new products to establishing
thought leadership to recruiting and retaining
talents for the future.

External innovation is building organizational
capabilities outside and around the organization so
that there is an enabling ecosystem and network to

complement, augment, and amplify internal innovation.

Organizational capabilities for internal and external innovation are distinct in many ways. We lay out the major differences between the two for easy understanding and to get you started. We believe that the following comparisons sift out the noise and give you what you must plan to accomplish if you are serious in building a holistic and powerful innovation ecosystem encompassing internal and external innovation engines.

	Internal Innovation	External Innovation
Objective	Build internal organizational capabilities to enable outcome-based innovation efforts.	Build organizational capabilities outside and around teams to accelerate internal innovation.
		(continued)

| **Key strategic activities to build organizational capability** | Build top-down and executive sponsorship with clear annual budget set aside for innovation activities.

Build a network of internal innovation champions who are departmental and functional leads to help push toward and execute on desired outcomes.

Narrow down the list of areas ripe for innovation that are also aligned with the strategy of the company.

The internal innovation of organizational capabilities is designed to be capable to quickly absorb insights from the external innovation ecosystem. | Identify the voice that the organization wants to convey in the external innovation ecosystem.

Align with the overarching corporate voice on strategy topics that matter to the organization.

Identify two or three key channels to help extend and expand the voice of the organization quickly so that external innovators know the organization, its openness to collaborate, and the focus areas of its innovation projects.
(continued) |

		Bring credibility by having dedicated expert to establish and nurture the external innovation ecosystem.
Measurement of success	Number of innovation projects that are on a path for long-term adoption with strong line of business support, functional support, and budget support. Each innovation project should clearly support one of the five key strategic outcomes.	Evaluate if the company timely participates in strategically important areas of innovation cultivated by external innovation ecosystem. Evaluate if the company shapes innovation discourse aligned to the 5 key innovation outcomes.
Talent Recruitment	Hire and retain an intrapreneur who has both strategy and operations	Hire and retain an intrapreneur similar to the profile of the

	experience. This individual is the ultimate "jack-of-all trades" and can embed himself or herself in any part of the organization. This individual can speak the language of the CEO, CFO, Engineering, Product, Marketing, and Sales. This individual does not take "no" for an answer inside the organization and is viewed as a rising leader.	internal innovation hire. He or she would be paired with a technologist if he or she does not have technical or product background. Marketing team would provide virtual support.

Emerging Technology Strategy

The second strategic area to build organizational capabilities is emerging technology strategy.

Emerging technology strategy explores the types of emerging technologies that can be and should be applied to empower outcome-based innovation. In parallel, emerging technology strategy is important because it helps design a path for organizations to adopt relevant emerging technologies efficiently (with minimal resources) and effectively (aligned with internal and external innovation agenda). In the long-term, the adoption of emerging technologies serves as a competitive advantage.

Technology is developing extremely fast and by definition dynamic. There are many different technologies that can be applied to help organizations arrive at similar outcomes. The main variables are cost and time. Therefore, having a strategic framework to identify and apply emerging technologies to business processes and growth initiatives is one of the most important activities for any CEO, CFO, or CTO.

Here, we will again discuss how to get started.

Here are the strategic questions to ask when you build out emerging technology strategy. The questions are divided into two types—a set of questions to gain clarity around current technology strategy and key stakeholders' decisions-making and a set of questions to gain insights into market intelligence on emerging technology strategy of customers, partners, and competitors.

Internal Ecosystem Assessment

- Does my organization have an enterprise technology strategy?

- How does the enterprise technology strategy map to a technology stack (hardware, software, applications, data)?

- What are the current technology teams wrestling with? Are they leaning toward building technology solutions internally? If so, why?

- What is the total IT budget? What accounts for 90% of the IT budget? What are the major IT vendors and IT outsourcing partners?

External Ecosystem Assessment

- What emerging technologies are top of mind and are potentially strategic and/or disruptive to existing customers?

- What emerging technologies are top of mind and potentially strategic and/or disruptive to existing competitors?

- What emerging technologies are top of mind and potentially strategic and/or disruptive to existing partners?

- What emerging technologies are being viewed as potentially transformative to large organizations in general?

- What organizational changes and regulatory changes could emerging technologies trigger and why?

Based on the answers to the questions, develop a perspective on the initial set of emerging technologies that the organization should focus on. Then take a multi-prong approach to establish a strategic framework and relevant workstreams to ensure that the team focusing on emerging technology strategy and innovation has the pulse on the various developments of emerging technologies. At the same time, the team needs to position the organization to jumpstart compelling research and development project and to readily capture commercial and technology partnership opportunities when such opportunities arise.

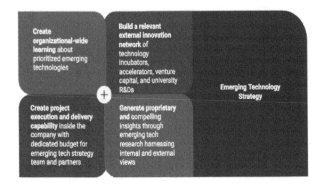

New Product Incubation

Another organizational innovation capability is new product incubation. We define new product incubation as a standalone and end-to-end process to create new product prototype aligned with business and emerging technology strategy. Equally important, having organizational capability for new product incubation is also to create a bridge between the internal assessment of an outcome-based innovation project around launching new product in adjacent or new market and the external validation of the project through organization's innovation ecosystem.

Many innovators and product managers will do well by following the new product framework. What we will point out here are two common pitfalls that could blindside innovators and product managers when they try to incubate new product ideas.

Pitfall #1

Corporate innovators focused on product incubation are siloed without much network in the rest of the organization. In many cases but not all, innovators with strong product incubation bent are excellent product individuals. They love breaking down ideas into product features and rally developers to build product prototypes. While this is an important skill, what is missing is building an early connection with other intrapreneurs, functional leads, and product development processes so that the product prototype from incubation can be further nurtured through additional complementary ways later on.

If you are an innovator, passionate and deft in product incubation, make sure that you create your own internal network of finance, marketing, project delivery, and corporate development colleagues who can be your "board of advocates and advisors" as you prepare to take your product prototype to the next step inside the organization.

Pitfall #2

Corporate innovators, unless they have some insights into corporate budgeting, often underestimate budget required to build a product prototype and continue the steps after prototype. These steps require budget for developers, product and user experience designs (UI/UX), and project delivery including building awareness inside and outside the organization. There are additional costs for education and continued refinement of the prototype before an incubated product can be launched by a line of business with dedicated resources for product development and management in the long run.

Market Development and Why Is It Important?

Market development is often forgotten in corporate innovation, but it is also another important element for succeeding in implementing practical and outcome-based innovation.

Market development is not sales. It is strategic business development for an early product or program that is on a two to three-year horizon to fully launch and scale.

Market noise always exists. In this case, one market noise is the uncertainty in how fast an emerging technology would mature and disrupt the current landscape. Market development helps bring a strong commercial lens and feedback to corporate innovators and intrapreneurs. Individuals working in market development need to team up with intrapreneurs to understand perspectives on similar innovation and emerging technology topics from customers, competitors, and partners and to bring the feedback into the organization to help further validate and clarify innovation ideas.

Making Startup Engagement Process Friendly

For many large organizations, collaborating with technology startups is no longer a "nice to have" motivated by a longing for innovation. Rather, it is a fundamental need required to accelerate a strategic and/or technology agenda. Building an organization capable of working with early stage companies is no easy task though. Least of all, it requires:

1. A strategic process of startup engagement for mutual value creation and capture.

2. An operational process that enables business units to onboard startup vendors or partners.

3. An experimentation mindset to develop continuous organizational learning and adoption.

*Create the strategic process of startup
engagement that allows for mutual value creation
and capture*

The first step of successfully working with startups is a clear strategic mandate and support from the top of an organization. Although it goes without saying, strategic alignment is a necessary prerequisite for setting the parameters of engagement and clarifying the models of collaboration that will allow the broader organization to understand how to work with startups.

Once strategic alignment is set, large enterprises need to define the specific business and technology areas of collaboration that could potentially yield the most mutual value creation in the long term.

From here, the enterprise needs to define a set of engagement models most appropriate for startups. For example, is it a pure vendor relationship, or is it something more? What parameters, outcomes, and milestones are the most important considerations for your organization? How do you map strategic projects with the right engagement model?

Some of these basic "soul-searching" questions can help guide the construction of a startup engagement model, which should then underpin the strategic process and the downstream considerations around the relationship.

Here are a few key examples:

Confidentiality: Not all engagement models require an NDA, and for those that do require more strict confidentiality terms, not all require an NDA upfront.

Length of the Engagement: The length of a vendor relationship is likely different from the length of a product innovation project. A pilot of an on-premise offering is different from a trial of a SaaS offering.

Assets Shared: Given the different capabilities offered by various startups, the assets and resources brought to bear by the enterprise will likely be different. Some require the availability of assets like access to an infrastructure environment, while others require the availability of an industry expert, a workflow specialist, or a set of APIs.

Intellectual Property: Have a clear definition of ownership of IP based on the expected outcome of the engagement. Some will have limited IP consideration and others will require a more detailed definition of IP up and down the stack. Know whether a startup can use the company logo or what the right case for co-branding is.

Milestones: Define milestones by categories of technology, commercial, and investment. Set milestones with the startup based on the agreed engagement model so that these mutually set goal posts that mirror the expected mutual value capture.

Create the operational processes that enable business units to onboard startups without too much friction

For large companies, once strategic buy-in and process are established, it is important to work with specific business units to help them understand a startup's perspective and pain points to build an operationalized process that allows for the cross-functional support of startups and various engagement models. The followings are Some examples of pain points to startups:

Long Contracts and Extensive Terms & Conditions: Challenge the functional areas to create a set of agreements for startups reflecting the most important and relevant terms specific to the engagement model. Identify the top most critical legal protection terms required for the company in working with a startup. Any other terms should be reviewed for limited relevance and put up for debate. Most engagements with startups do not merit long contracts given the initial scope of the collaboration.

Decentralized Contracting Process: Work with all functional areas to define a centralized contracting process for startups. Ideally, there should be only one agreement containing universal terms. As engagements evolve, addendum can be incorporated to reflect the specific natures of various engagement.

Lack of Transparency to Startups: Build a collective mindset and effort with functional owners to provide as much detail as possible to startups on how the contracting process works in the company to set the right expectation. This helps startups plan and stay focused on course with the established process.

The first step is helping colleagues understand why certain business processes can be cumbersome for startups. Then, be a close partner to these colleagues to understand their business concerns, performance measurements, and operational parameters. From here, with a holistic understanding, identify and suggest changes to the status quo while striving to maintain the most valued elements by functional areas.

Colleagues in procurement, legal, technology, product management, and marketing need to recognize that their respective areas need to develop function-specific processes to cater to a "new" class of vendors and/or partners that do not have the profiles of their large clients.

With this context and conditioning, work with legal and procurement to create "short form and lean" documents that address the most pertinent operational parameters for the current phase of the engagement, with the recognition on both sides that, as the collaboration expands into the next phase, the contract may expand and more parameters may need to be addressed.

*Experimentation to develop continuous
organizational learning and adoption*

Lastly, in many cases, collaboration with startups starts on a small scale to allow room for mutual learning, fine tuning, pivoting, and synchronization for further joint efforts if the first proof-of-concept or phase of collaboration proves successful.

Many of the standard terms & conditions for larger clients are superfluous initially. By enforcing the status quo on startup engagements, large enterprises miss the mark on the strategic imperative to work with startups in the first place.

The better way is to hone-in-on the absolute minimum parameters needed for cross functional engagement with startups and let the experiment with startups run with close monitoring.

Learn from the startup engagements and assess whether the operational parameters in place are sufficient. With iteration, the operational process and legal documents created to help govern collaboration with startups can and will become the broadly accepted practice in the enterprise. Only by this will an environment for mutual value creation and capture with the most compelling startups be ultimately enabled.

CHAPTER 5

EMPLOYEE DEVELOPMENT & BUILDING INNOVATION CULTURE

This chapter is devoted to building innovation culture.

Despite what people tell you, building innovation culture is a hard-to-measure activity, especially for companies that have significant workforce and legacy infrastructures.

While a number of well-known innovation building practices exist, we present a different view of building innovation culture. We hope that as you build innovation culture inside your organization, you can pause and think about alternative approaches rather than adopting an existing model in your organization since "that is what others are doing."

Being innovative is a state of being for an organization. As we know, a company that does not constantly innovate to drive impactful outcomes in the long term will eventually become uncompetitive and lose shareholder value. Being innovative is a continuous effort that every employee of the company should demonstrate, starting with the CEO.

Making innovation the DNA of an organization and of every employee is incredibly difficult. Existing or new employees are unlikely to be truly innovative in their work if enabling organizational and incentive structures are not in place. This is a major challenge faced by many medium-sized and large organizations today.

The CEO is the Chief Innovation Officer

Many organizations have begun to hire Chief Innovation Officers to build innovation culture. We challenge this approach. In fact, we believe that the CEO of every organization should also be the Chief Innovation Officer.

It is the job and strategic mandate of a CEO to create innovation strategy and instill a culture of innovation in the organization with his or her management team. It is the strategic mandate of a CEO to ultimately put innovation in practice at every level of the organization. Having a designated Chief Innovation Officer creates additional intermediary to innovation and removes the CEO from having direct accountability in building innovation culture.

Practically, what do we mean by the notion that a CEO is also the Chief Innovation Officer?

We mean the following.

The CEO should have specific milestones and performance measurements associated with his or her compensation to drive outcome-based innovation forward as outlined in previous chapters. His or her team should also carry the same milestones and performance measurements. And the same milestones and performance measurements should be further assigned to the rest of the organization so that everyone in the firm, from the CEO to the entry-level new hire, feels a sense of responsibility to innovate on a defined set of strategic outcomes that matter to the organization.

Therefore, if you are building a chief innovation officer role inside the company, pause and think about the bigger picture. Are you doing this just to check a box or are you truly starting to build innovation DNA into the organization?

Allocating 20% of the employee time to innovation is not realistic for most companies

Companies that replicate the much discussed Google innovation model by enabling employees to spend 20% of their time on innovation projects need to think twice. Google's culture is very hard to replicate; no company is like Google.

Replicating innovation process by allocating a portion of employee's time to innovation often does not work because employees in most companies do not have that additional capacity or the organizational support to do more. As a consequence, an innovation project becomes either a night job or a responsibility for individuals who can devote more time to go the extra mile. This can be problematic. For instance, the employee with a "micro-manager" boss may not be able to work on the innovation project. Working mothers might find this challenging because they simply do not have additional 25% of the time outside their roles to focus on innovation even if they believe that they are capable of making an impact.

To prevent creating wrong organizational structure and incentives for outcome-based innovation, take away this practice of allocating a percentage of employee's time for innovation. Rather than using time as a way to manage the workforce's ability to innovate, embed relevant performance metrics associated with making progress on outcome-based innovation. Leave time allocation to employee's discretion and let performance metrics drive behavior from management to staff. This way, the organization is structured to embed innovation as an essential part of the role, not as an extracurricular activity.

If an employee works in Sales, an outcome-based innovation performance metric could be proposing new ways to reduce churn in sales team. Another example could be redefining the sales operations process so that it is more technology enabled, resulting in more time for sales representatives to actually sell and stay in front of potential customers.

If an employee works in Research and Development or in engineering, an outcome-based innovation performance milestone could be drafting an impactful product idea through partnership with a colleague in the business unit.

The impact of the product idea could be evaluated by its alignment to the strategic roadmap of the company, in the context of where the industry is moving. Another example could be identifying an adjacent technology and suggesting ways in which the technology could be relevant to and applied by external customers of the organization.

If an employee works in Financial Planning and Accounting, an outcome-based innovation performance metric could be identifying a process improvement or a new key performance indicator (KPI) or a better way to visualize operational metrics to help further understand the business.

The above examples show that innovating is and can be part of the job. It is up to the organization to allow employees innovate in their jobs. If a milestone or performance metric is appropriately designed and established as part of the overall annual or semi-annual performance objective of the employee recognition, then the organization would see an increased probability that the employee will innovate for outcome. This is how innovation DNA is engendered and sustained in practice.

The examples above also exemplify that innovation DNA with the right design and execution model can create engaged employees and mobilize them to think about the broader impact of their respective roles and to develop the "bigger picture."

In parallel, having outcome-based innovation as part of the role stretches employees to think deeper, broader, and more collaboratively. This practice enhances talent development for the organization and allows organizations to nurture and develop employees who can potentially move into other functional roles. When done right, this strategy creates a positive cycle where employees gain new skills through innovation projects in their current jobs, and these new skills in turn are transferable to other job functions inside the company.

Creating enabling organizational processes to help employees innovate in their roles and maximize outcomes in the innovation process

Complementing outcome-based innovation milestones and performance metrics for employees should be a set of organizational processes. These processes help employees achieve these said milestones and performance metrics. The following examples of organizational processes will effectively enable employees in their innovation journey.

A fast-track Innovation Funding Program

Employees will be able to submit proposals for corporate funding, no string attached. Many companies with innovation programs have this process, but the key is to have this process adjacent to setting employee-level metrics on innovation as core part of employee's roles. These innovation "starter funds" to further activate innovation DNA do not have to be big. They can be as small as $5000 to $10,000 for each project.

An Innovation Knowledge and Resource Exchange

Employees will be able to share innovation projects including both best practices and failures with other colleagues. The virtual innovation knowledge exchange essentially provides crowdsourced insights into innovation successes, challenges, and ways to overcome roadblocks for employees. Such exchange shows another dimension of organization's commitment to innovate by providing actual enabling process to help employees reach their outcome-based innovation goals.

An Innovation Mentorship System

Employees are matched with other colleagues who have successfully delivered outcome-based innovation projects and met their goals in previous years. This mentor matching is implemented regardless of levels and hierarchy. The mentors can be individuals who are known as optimistic change agents. The mentors can also be the highly resourceful employees who can help colleagues overcome challenges. The mentors can also be individuals known as "relationship connectors" who can connect colleagues to other parts of the organizations effectively. Whatever the mentor-mentee match may be, the important element is to institute another cross-organizational process to provide day-to-day support for employees who are on innovation journeys. The goal of the innovation mentorship system is to help intrapreneurs maximize probability of success in their outcome-based innovation projects. The innovation mentorship system also helps to increase employee engagement through organic cross-organizational learning and professional development.

CHAPTER 6

KEEP IT SIMPLE

In reality, companies that build and sell enterprise software and emerging technologies have to navigate through complex organizations, complex sales cycles, complex procurement, and sometimes complex implementation for a complex system and infrastructure to get the job done.

Our cognitive biases tend to drive us to communicate what we are trying to build or sell through a complex lens because mostly our brains recall or retrieve what we experienced or encountered directly and easily.

It sounds basic, but I believe a key ingredient of enterprise startup success is to simplify, simplify, and simplify. If you are building a product or a new business inside the organization, "keep it simple" also applies to you as an intrapreneur.

Simplify the mission statement and value proposition of what you are building so that anyone and everyone can understand in an instant what you are building and why it really matters. This should be done in 2-3 sentences.

Simplify strategy to enable the value proposition so that every minute spent building the product or business is around this strategy. And this core strategy drives everything else you do.

Simplify your product. The goal is not to build as much as you can; the goal is to create real value.

Simplify marketing channel (external or inside an organization) to test one or two hypotheses at a given time to ensure that you truly understand what works and what does not.

Simplify sales process but make the process rigorous with cadence, onboarding, training, and proper compensation model that aligns incentive to performance.

Simplify pricing. If you have to spend more than three sentences explaining pricing, then your customer will have a hard time figuring out how to budget for the product at scale.

CHAPTER 7

BUILDING A BUSINESS IS RUNNING A MARATHON

I finished the New York City Marathon in November 2018, my 13th marathon. As someone who has been doing endurance sports for years, I see many aspects of endurance sports relevant to business building. No surprising that many people say that building business and innovation is not a sprint but a marathon.

But what does that really mean?

The first big lesson that I have learned about running a marathon is applying consistency to the overall strategy throughout the 26.2 miles. No matter which training program a runner uses, consistently applying what works is the most important strategic and tactical step. If a runner runs at a certain pace at the marathon, the right strategy for him or her is to be able to keep a consistent pace.

If a runner runs and then walks 20 steps, then he or she should do that after each mile or after every 3 miles. If a runner needs to have milestones in between, he or she may consistently give high-fives to kids at the end of a mile.

Hence, whatever the set of activities a runner does to get to the finish line, practicing consistency is essential to develop and sustain physical and mental strength to run through the finish line.

In building a business or innovation project, management team often hears from the Board of Directors to find repeatability or success factors in enterprise sales, user acquisition, product marketing, talent retention, etc.

Drawing a parallel to running a marathon, the management team needs to identify methods, frameworks, business practices that the company can apply consistently across teams, customer scenarios, and marketing. Build consistency into the strategic and operating fabric.

The second big lesson that I have learned is having a roadmap to finish. A runner who has run more than one marathon typically knows the activities that work both well and consistently. An experienced runner also knows how to execute along the journey from mile 0 to mile 26 with a roadmap: stop at a station to get water at mile 7, 10, 15; listen to playlist #3 that has a certain tempo between miles 13 and 17; and deploy a specific strategy to get through the last 4-6 miles.

Likewise, in building business or innovation project, a roadmap is a necessity. Many companies are good at building technology roadmaps because technology roadmaps are based on near-term and long-term features that would be built.

In contrast, many companies struggle with building operating roadmaps to get to the ultimate strategic goal. Analogous to running a marathon, companies need to know if an enterprise sales cycle is expected to be 10 month long, what company should do at 2-month mark, 6-month mark, 8-month mark, who is going to be the "runner" and who is going to be at the "water station,", and what techniques they should adopt to keep the momentum.

The third lesson that I have learned is to avoid overconfidence and the herd mentality. Many runners who do not finish or who get injured along the way are often those who run too fast for the first half of the race or who forgot who they are (as runners) because they go with the crowd and herd of excited runners. Being overconfident and following the herd make a runner step into potholes, lose stamina too early, or more likely feel depleted when he or she is no longer with the big herd.

Similarly, innovators need to avoid the same overconfidence and herd mentality. Overconfidence and herd mentality make a management team miss opportunities, unable to remediate mistakes, or forget to focus on the basic set of values or DNA that makes the company differentiated.

CHAPTER 8

MANAGING CHAOS

A year or so ago, Reid Hoffman, founder of LinkedIn, wrote a thought-provoking piece about managing chaos and enabling innovation. He also asked his community to share their thoughts by posing the following questions:

How do you manage chaos? Can you think of a time when allowing your team "a dash of insubordination" enabled your company to be more innovative?

Here are my thoughts:

Having built leadership experience in various functions and new business ventures at both IBM and Thomson Reuters, I believe that corporations do know that in order for innovation to "bubble up," employees need to (1) see and feel a culture of innovation, (2) be given flexibility to devote time to thinking about problems outside his or her immediate mandate (and not get penalized for it), and (3) receive clear message from the senior management to rest of the organization hat innovation is a core part of the company, not a fleeting thing or a nice-to-have.

While many companies still need to do better in cultivating a culture to encourage innovation, I believe that given the external market pressure and increasing recognition that technology is changing the status quo and existing assumptions, a good number of companies have built or are building an innovation culture that is encouraging more open debates and employee channels to generate ideas and get feedback.

The key challenge is the first question—how does a company manage chaos?

Here is my interpretation of the question: when employees are given the platform and sometimes even the opportunity to get budget to innovate for better processes or new products, how does a company create working principles and a set of efficient processes to manage good types of chaos (innovation ideas) which can drive actual business outcome in the future? I have been on the practitioner and recipient end of this "managing chaos." Things that work and can help manage good types of chaos:

- Have a clear process to employees on how the innovation projects can be moved from a groundswell effort to a potentially funded effort that will be actively incubated and protected by the company without dependency to any business unit's P&L for funding in the near term.

- Walk the talk by funding some of the innovation projects—a.k.a. demonstrate to employees in practice that the "chaos" (innovation) funnel is indeed working.

- Innovation KPIs, when measured correctly, can be powerful enablers to allow employees to more efficiently and effectively self-organize on innovation projects and to better understand what the innovation journey requires. Also, innovation KPIs enable employees to generate more promising innovation ideas. And it is not solely about coming up with ideas for the sake of coming up cool ideas. A business needs good ideas that can be implemented through iterations so that eventually these ideas drive strategic outcomes. If they don't, stop in between iterations and stop wasting resources. Train employees to learn how to think critically and to differentiate a bad idea, a good idea, and an impactful one.

- Build technology literacy through all ranks of management so that when an innovation idea is raised, it will not be immediately stifled or ignored by a manager who may have limited market awareness or technology literacy to be capable to take a keen interest.

- Identify employee leaders (not necessarily managers) who can champion best practices on how to think about innovation in different parts of the organization so that the management of "chaos" can be scaled, and the funnel of innovation ideas becomes a humming engine.

CHAPTER 9

CHECKLIST FOR SUCCESS

This chapter offers a practical innovator's checklist, a set of questions that an intrapreneur should ask and work through as he or she builds out an outcome-based innovation project.

Though building innovation is not rocket science, it does require tactical planning and critical thinking for the long-term success. Not everyone succeeds at building innovation.

The checklist, while short, contains the most important questions for intrapreneurs. It provides a handy and practical guide for any individual who is keen to deliver an innovation project methodically and effectively. The checklist can be used for individuals in existing organizations or individuals joining new organizations.

The answers to most of these questions demand you to deconstruct organization focus, patterns, motivations, and strengths and weaknesses, which in turn help you understand where you can add significant value to the organization.

- Has your organization hired a Chief Innovation Officer?

- If the answer is yes, what are the priorities of the Chief Innovation Officer?

- Is the mandate of the Chief Innovation Officer to execute on innovation projects or to build thought leadership or both?

- How is the leader measured quantitatively based on a clear set of business objectives?

- How is the corporate strategy team engaged in innovation projects across the organization?

- Does your organization have a corporate venture team? If yes, how is the corporate venture team structured?

- And what are the strategic priorities of the corporate venture team?

- What are the focus areas of the current innovation teams according to your observation?

- Who are the current intrapreneurs in the company?

- What innovation projects are underway?

- Who are the business sponsors of these projects?

- What are organizational funding sources for innovation projects?

- Is there a technology infrastructure to share innovation projects across the organization?

- What are mission-critical processes inside the organization that are relevant to you?

- What are the major pain points that you find within those processes?

- Does your organization have any innovation projects to help address the pain points of mission-critical processes? If yes, are those innovation projects outcome-based based on this book's framework?

- What relevant market trends have emerged or are emerging in your organization? Why are those market trends relevant to your organization? Who are sharing those market trends internally?

- What is the orientation of your organization's innovation projects? Big plays or operational focused?

- Based on your research, can you provide additional insights and help further refine or strengthen innovation projects to increase their probabilities to succeed?

- Within your performance measurement plan, do you have performance metrics to take on outcome-based innovation projects? If no, how can you influence your manager and your second-line manager to agree to incorporate the said innovation performance metrics in your annual performance plan?

- Do you have both internal and external network to enable your outcome-based innovation efforts? If yes, how can you become an enabler for others so that the entire internal innovation community of the organization grows organically under your leadership?

- Have you developed a cadence to record your research on innovation ideas and apply the frameworks discussed in the earlier chapters of this book to each of the emerging innovation ideas?

Good luck for being a change maker who implements outcome-based innovation!

Small and large organizations need you.

ABOUT THE AUTHOR

Joyce Shen is a recognized executive and thought leader in business and technology with deep operating and investing experience. Joyce is a published author, frequent speaker, and advisor on emerging technologies, new product innovation & development, and corporate strategy. She is an institutional investor in enterprise software and big data companies. Joyce is also a faculty of data science at UC Berkeley. Joyce was previously the global managing director of emerging technologies and venture investments in the CTO office at Thomson Reuters where she built and led global emerging tech partnerships program and the emerging technology venture fund. Before Thomson Reuters, Joyce was the founding global CFO of IBM Cloud Platform. She also spent several years in IBM Corporate Development leading acquisitions and divestitures.

Joyce received her undergraduate and masters degrees from the University of Chicago. Joyce lives in New York City.

INDEX

acquisition, 15
autonomous model, 28, 29, 30
Autonomous model, 28

board of advocates and advisors, 53
business development, 23, 54
business processes, 21, 48, 60

CEO, 19, 24, 29, 38, 39, 46, 48, 64, 65
CFO, 16, 19, 22, 24, 29, 38, 39, 46, 48, 90
checklist, 85
Chief Innovation Officer, iii, 65, 86
clarification, 5, 7, 16, 18, 21, 23
client insights, 23
cognitive biases, 74
confirmation bias, 4
corporate development, 32, 33, 53
corporate strategy, 25
corporate venture, 27, 28, 29, 30, 31, 32, 33, 35, 36, 37, 39, 41, 87

corporate ventures, 27, 31, 32
cross-organizational learning, 73

embedded model, 33
emerging technologies, ii, 47, 48, 49, 50, 74, 90
external innovation, 43

financial funding, 10
financial sponsor, 8, 9
five categories of outcomes, 14
five types of outcomes, 34

herd mentality, 80
human resources, 25, 26, 30, 38

innovation culture, 63, 64, 65, 82
innovation DNA, 66, 69, 71
innovation ecosystem, 36, 40, 41, 43, 44, 45, 46, 52
innovation funding program, 71
innovation mentorship, 72
intellectual property, 23

intellectual property, 38, 58
internal innovation, 43
intrapreneur, ii, 35, 37, 46, 74, 85

keep it simple, 74
key performance indicator, 69
KPIs, 83

leadership, 0, 2, 14, 22, 23, 24, 34, 35, 36, 43, 81, 86, 89
line of business, 25

manage chaos, 81, 82
marathon, 0, 77
market development, 17, 18, 19, 23, 42, 54
market development strategy, 17, 19
marketing, 38, 46, 47
mergers and acquisitions, 17
minimal viable product, 5, 7, 8, 9, 10
MVP, 5, 8, 11

NDA, 57
new product incubation, 42, 51

organizational processes, 70
organizational support, 16, 19, 67
outcome-based innovation, 1
overconfidence, 80

P&L, 83, 90
performance measurement, 24, 89
performance measurements, 60, 65
performance metrics, 67, 70, 89
post-investment performance, 38
product prototype, 51, 53
professional development, 73
project delivery, 10, 53
proof-of-concept, 3, 61

recruiting strategy, 16, 19
research and development, 68
risk management, 21
roadmap, 16, 18, 19, 68, 79
SaaS, 57
sales, 38, 46, 68
sales operations, 68

strategic minority
     investment, 28
strategic partnerships, 38
synchronization, 7, 8, 16,
     18, 21, 23

talent pipeline, 14, 24, 26,
     35
technology infrastructure,
     87
technology partnership,
     50

technology strategy, 25,
     26, 42, 47, 48, 49, 50,
     51

UI/UX, 53

validation, 3, 4, 16, 18,
     21, 23
validation, clarification,
     and synchronization, 3,
     13
vendor relationship, 56,
     57

ALSO BY JOYCE J. SHEN

Blockchain in Financial Markets and Beyond: The Promises and Limitations of Blockchain: Taking Stock and Lessons Learned

29640393R00066

Made in the USA
Lexington, KY
01 February 2019